Cherokee Mythology

Captivating Myths and Legends of a Native American Tribe

Free Bonus from Captivating History
(Available for a Limited time)

Hi History Lovers!

Now you have a chance to join our exclusive history list so you can get your first history ebook for free as well as discounts and a potential to get more history books for free! Simply visit the link below to join.

Captivatinghistory.com/ebook

Also, make sure to follow us on Facebook, Twitter and Youtube by searching for Captivating History.

Contents

Introduction

The Cherokee are an Indigenous American tribe whose lands were originally in the southeastern part of what is now the United States. However, they appear to have settled there after migrating from lands further north. The Cherokee language is in the Iroquoian language family and has its own writing system: a syllabary developed in the early nineteenth century by Sequoyah, a Cherokee man, who worked as a blacksmith and silversmith. He wanted to create a means by which his people could read and write in their language.

The earliest contact between the Cherokee and Europeans appears to have been the 1540 arrival in Tennessee of Hernando de Soto. In 1567, another Spanish group attempted to settle in Cherokee lands but were rebuffed. Settlements by Scottish, Irish, and English colonists could not be dislodged, though, and the Cherokee began losing their native lands to white settlers, with devastating consequences to the tribe. The settlers brought diseases to which the Indigenous peoples had no immunity, and the deaths that ensued significantly diminished the Cherokee population. In 1835, the Cherokee were rounded up and forced to march from their homes in the Southeastern United States to the Oklahoma Territory, where they were put on reservations. The Trail of Tears was a major traumatic event for the Cherokee; not only did they lose their homes and their lands, but many people died from the hardships of the march, while others took their own lives rather than allow themselves to continue to live under the domination of white colonists.

In the twentieth century, the conversion of the Oklahoma Territory into the state of Oklahoma in 1907 led to a dismantling of much of the infrastructure the Cherokee had built to govern themselves and educate their children, including the loss of some reservation lands to a new generation of white settlers. It was not until the 1960s that the Cherokee began to regroup and reorganize themselves as a nation, which culminated with the ratification of a new tribal Constitution in 1975. Today, the Cherokee people continue to occupy reservation lands in Oklahoma, where they practice Indigenous foodways and medicine and engage in traditional pastimes such as stickball—a game similar to lacrosse.

In Cherokee myth—as in other Indigenous American traditions—the whole of creation is alive and able to communicate like humans and with the human beings who share their environment. Cherokee myths explain how the world came to be the way it is, and impart important lessons about Cherokee cultural values. In the brief collection of stories retold in this volume, you will learn why the opossum has no fur on its tail, how the bat and the flying fox were created, and how medicine and disease came to afflict human beings, while the misfortunes and desires of animals and birds become expressions of important Cherokee cultural values, such as modesty of speech, humility, and gratitude for the earth's bounty. Like the human beings with whom they share their world, the animals and birds play stickball and hold dances, and they have councils in townhouses—communal spaces that were an important part of Cherokee settlements.

These stories are very old—passed down from generation to generation by storytellers who wished to instruct, entertain, and keep their traditions alive. They are part of a living tradition; the cultural fabric of an Indigenous American people who have survived against terrible odds, continue to live according to their traditional values and wish to create a better future for themselves and their children.

Why the Possum's Tail is Bare

Everyone knows that the opossum has a bare tail today—it is long, pink, and hairless. However, it was not always that way. Once, Possum's tail was covered in long, luxurious fur, and Possum was very proud of it. Possum was always singing about how beautiful his tail was and showing it off at dances, and every morning he sat outside his lodge and combed his tail until the fur shone in the sun.

Rabbit soon became very tired of Possum showing off his fine tail.

"That Possum," Rabbit said. "Always bragging about his tail, and waving it about in the air, and combing it where everyone can see. Someone needs to take him down a peg."

Now, Rabbit was jealous of Possum's tail because Rabbit only had a small, stubby tail. This was because Rabbit once argued with Bear, and Bear pulled off Rabbit's fine, long tail. Everyone knew what had happened to Rabbit, and he couldn't stand to be reminded of what a lovely tail he'd had before Bear got his paws on it. Rabbit decided that he would play a trick on Possum—a trick that would stop him singing and bragging about his tail forever.

Not long after Rabbit decided to play his trick, the animals decided it was time for them to have a great council and dance. Rabbit was the messenger, so he went to each of the animals and told them when the council and dance would be held.

When Rabbit came to Possum's lodge and told him about the council and dance, Possum said, "Well, I guess I'll come, but I'll only be there if I have a special seat out in front. I want to spread out my lovely tail so that everyone can admire it."

"Oh, I think that can be arranged," Rabbit said. "And I'll not only make sure you get the best seat—I'll even send someone to help you comb your tail so that it will be the most beautiful thing anyone has ever seen."

"That is splendid!" Possum said. "I will surely come to the council now. I can't wait to show off my tail!"

"Oh, you're going to show it off all right," Rabbit said to himself as he hopped away from Possum's lodge. "Just not in the way you think."

Next, Rabbit went to Cricket's lodge. He invited Cricket to the council and dance and asked him to help with a little trick he had planned.

"I'll certainly come to the council and dance," Cricket said. "Tell me what you have in mind for your trick, and I'll see to it that it gets done."

Rabbit told Cricket what to do, and then he hopped away to tell the rest of the animals about the council.

In the morning, Cricket went to Possum's lodge. Possum was already sitting outside and had just begun to comb his tail.

"Good morning, Possum," Cricket said. "My, what a lovely tail you have! Someone should help you get it ready for the council this evening. It would be a shame if it weren't absolutely perfect when everyone sees it."

"Just so," Possum said. "Would you be willing to help?"

"Certainly!" Cricket said, and so Possum handed Cricket his comb and then laid down and closed his eyes to enjoy having his tail combed by someone else.

Cricket combed out Possum's tail so that it shone even more brightly than it ever had before. When he was done, he said to Possum, "It would be a shame if any little bit of fur came out of place before the council. What if I tied it up so that it stays just as perfect as it is now? You can remove the threads when you get to the council place and show everyone your perfect tail."

"That is a splendid idea, Cricket!" Possum said. "Please do tie up my tail."

Cricket got some fine thread and began wrapping it around Possum's tail. But as he did so, he snipped off every last hair at the roots. Cricket did this so gently that Possum didn't notice at all, and the thread held everything in place, so the tail looked as it always did, except wrapped up in thread.

That evening, Possum went to the council, his tail still wrapped up in the thread. Rabbit greeted him and showed him to a special seat, just as he had promised. Soon it came time for Possum to dance. He pulled the thread off his tail, but he was so intent on dancing his very best and showing off his tail that he didn't notice all the fur falling to the ground, leaving his tail as bare as bare could be.

Possum went into the center of the circle and began to dance and sing.

"My tail is the most beautiful," he sang, not noticing that all the other animals were shouting at him because they had seen all the fur fall off his tail.

Possum sang and danced some more.

"My tail has the most shining fur. The fur has the best color."

Again, the animals shouted at Possum, but he still didn't notice.

"Look at my tail!" Possum sang. "It's the best tail in the world!"

Finally, Possum had to stop singing and pay attention to the other animals because now the animals were all laughing so hard at Possum's bare tail that their sides hurt.

Possum looked down, and instead of a beautiful tail covered in soft, fine fur, there was this naked thing without a single hair on it. It looked just like a lizard's tail! Possum was astonished and very ashamed. So much so that he couldn't even finish his dance. Instead, he flopped down on the ground and rolled over onto his back, with a grin on his face. And that is why opossums now roll over and play dead if they are caught by surprise.

Kanati and Selu

Kanati and Selu were man and wife, and they lived very happily together. Kanati's name meant "Lucky Hunter," and every time he went out to hunt, he came home with something good to eat. Selu's name meant "Corn," and she grew many good things in her garden. Selu also prepared the meat that Kanati brought home. When she was done butchering it, she would go to the river and wash the blood off the meat in the flowing water.

Kanati and Selu had one child, a son. The boy was quite young and spent most of his days playing in the woods near his family's home, or along the riverbank. For several days in a row, Kanati and Selu heard their son laughing and talking with someone down near the river. It sounded like he was playing with another child, but no other families were living nearby.

Finally, the boy's parents decided to find out what was going on.

Kanati asked him, "Who is it that you play with every day, down near the river?"

"Oh, there's another little boy there," the child said. "He comes up out of the river. He says he's my older brother, but his mother threw him away. When we are done playing, he goes back into the river."

When Kanati and Selu heard this, they knew exactly where the strange boy was from. He had been born from the blood that Selu had washed into the river when she prepared the meat that Kanati brought home.

For the next few days, Kanati and Selu tried to get a glimpse of the boy that came out of the river, but he always managed to slip away right before they arrived.

Kanati then went to his son and said, "Next time the boy from the river comes to play with you, tell him that you want to wrestle with him. While you are wrestling, wrap your arms tight around him and hold him fast. When you have him pinned, call me, and I will come to you."

In the morning, Kanati and Selu's son went down by the river to play, as he always did. Kanati and Selu waited near the lodge to see whether their son would call for them. Sure enough, they soon heard their child calling loudly for his father. Kanati and Selu ran down to the riverbank. There they saw their son holding tightly to another child, who was about the same size as their boy. The other child was trying hard to get away, but Kanati and Selu's son quickly held him.

When the child from the river saw Selu, he shouted, "Leave me alone! Let me go! You didn't want me. You threw me away. You threw me into the river!"

Kanati and Selu took the strange river boy by the hand and dragged him back to their lodge. Because he seemed always to want to escape, Kanati and Selu kept him locked inside the lodge.

After many days, the child from the river began to calm down and seemed willing to live with his new family. Kanati and Selu adopted him as their son and called him Wild Boy. But even though Wild Boy stopped trying to escape, his nature was still untamed, and he frequently got up to mischief, coming up with cunning plans and getting his brother to help him carry them out.

One day, Wild Boy and his brother sat together on the riverbank.

Wild Boy said, "Father always brings home game every morning. He never comes home empty-handed. But I've never once seen a deer or turkey or rabbit anywhere around here. I wonder where the animals come from?"

"I don't know," Wild Boy's brother said. "He never told me, and I've never asked."

"Let's follow him tomorrow," Wild Boy said. "I want to find out where all that meat comes from."

In the morning, Kanati went out to hunt as usual. The boys pretended to be uninterested in where their father was going, but as soon as they thought he wouldn't notice them following, they crept along the path behind him. They followed until Kanati entered a swamp.

Wild Boy said to his brother, "Stay here. I'm going to go with Father."

Then Wild Boy changed himself into a bit of bird's down and alighted on Kanati's shoulder. Wild Boy rode along until Kanati stopped at a pond where some reeds were growing. Kanati picked some of the reeds and fixed arrowheads and feathers to them to make arrows. When he had enough arrows, he walked out of the swamp.

At the edge of the swamp, the wind rose, blowing Wild Boy in his bird-down shape off his father's shoulder.

Wild Boy then took his human form again and went to find his brother.

"What did you find?" the other boy asked when Wild Boy arrived at the place he was hiding.

"I'm not sure," Wild Boy said. "Father took some reeds and put some feathers on one end and something pointy on the other. I don't know what those are for, but I want to find out. Come on—I know which way Father went. We can probably still follow him if we're quick."

The boys soon found their father's trail and could see him walking steadily up the mountain through the trees. The boys walked as quietly as they could and kept well out of sight.

Finally, Kanati came to a place where the mountain's stone face rose into the sky, and where there were many large rocks piled against it. Kanati moved one of the large rocks aside, and out sprang a deer. Kanati nocked an arrow to his bow and shot the deer. Then he closed up the hole in the mountain, put the deer on his shoulders, and headed for home.

"Look at that!" Wild Boy said. "He just comes here, lets an animal out, kills it, and then comes home. That's why he's such a good hunter—he has all the game shut inside the mountain."

"Yes," Wild Boy's brother said, "but if we don't get home before he does, he'll be suspicious, and we'll both be in terrible trouble if he finds out that we followed him today."

"True," Wild Boy said. "Let's run. I know a shortcut through the forest."

The boys ran as fast as they could and arrived home just moments before their father.

"Why are you both so out of breath?" Kanati said when he saw the boys panting in front of the lodge.

"Oh, we just had a race to see who could get from the river to home the fastest," said Wild Boy. "I won, of course."

The boys waited for a few days before going back to the hole where the animals were held. They waited until their parents weren't watching and then followed the trail their father had taken through the forest and up the mountain. They found the stone that covered the hole and moved it aside. Suddenly, out of the hole streamed hundreds and hundreds of animals and birds. Deer, raccoons, opossums, and rabbits went jumping and running past. Turkeys, pigeons, pheasants, and all manner of other birds flew out of the hole and into the trees. The boys covered the hole back up, but by the time they had rolled the heavy stone back into place, it was too late. All the birds and animals had gone.

Back at the lodge, Kanati heard a noise like thunder coming from the direction of the mountain. He looked up and saw great clouds of birds flying up into the sky and scattering in every direction. Kanati called for his children, but they didn't answer. Then Kanati knew what had happened: his naughty boys had followed him one day and found the hole where he kept the birds and animals. Kanati ran to the place where the hole was, arriving just as the boys were putting the stone back over the hole.

Kanati said nothing to the two boys, who stood next to the hole, hanging their heads in shame. Kanati moved the stone aside and went into the hole. Inside the hole were four large jars, covered tightly with lids. Kanati kicked over the jars one by one, and out of the jars came all kinds of insects. Fleas, lice, wasps, hornets, and biting gnats came streaming out of the hole. Many of them alit on the boys and began to sting and bite them. Kanati did nothing; he allowed the boys to be punished by the stings and the bites.

When he thought they had suffered enough, Kanati chased away the insects and sat the boys down to talk.

"What you have done is very bad indeed," he said. "Before you opened the hole, all I had to do was come up here and let out an animal or a bird or two, and then we'd have plenty to eat. But now that you've let out all the birds and animals, I won't be able to get them back in there. From now on, when we hunt, we'll have to go looking for game, and there might be some days when we don't find any. Go home now, and try to stay out of trouble. I'll see whether I can catch something for dinner, but that might not be possible."

The boys went home, not saying a word to each other all the long way back to the lodge. When they arrived, they were very tired and hungry.

"Is there anything to eat, Mother?" Wild Boy said.

"There is no meat because Father hasn't come back from hunting yet," Selu said. "But maybe I can cook you something else. Rest here while I go find some food." Then Selu picked up a basket and left the lodge.

"I wonder where she gets all the grain, fruit, and vegetables she serves us." Wild Boy said. "Maybe we should follow her and find out."

"Haven't you learned anything?" Wild Boy's brother said. "You just watch: If we follow her and see what happens wherever it is that she goes, something horrible will happen, just like it happened with the animals and birds. And then we'll really be hungry."

"Maybe something will happen, maybe it won't," Wild Boy said. "You don't have to come with me if you're so frightened. I can find things out by myself."

In the end, Wild Boy's brother went along because he was stung by being called a coward. The two boys crept after their mother, who walked through the forest carrying the empty basket.

Finally, she arrived at a storehouse that had but one door and no windows, and that had been built upon tall stilts so that the animals couldn't get into it. Selu climbed up the ladder and went into the storehouse with her basket. Once she had gone inside, the boys followed and picked a hole in the clay that had been used to caulk between the logs that made the floor of the storehouse.

"Why, it's completely empty!" Wild Boy whispered to his brother.

"That is certainly strange," the other boy said, who couldn't see as well into the room as Wild Boy could. "What is she doing now?"

"She's rubbing her belly. Oh!"

"What happened?"

"When she rubbed her belly, the basket filled halfway with corn! Wait, she's rubbing under her armpits now. Oh!" Wild Boy said.

"What happened this time?"

"The other half of the basket filled up with beans!"

"How is that even possible?"

"I think our mother must be a witch," Wild Boy said. "We mustn't eat anything out of that basket. It's surely poisonous."

"What are we going to do?"

"Right now, we're going to get down and hide because Mother is getting ready to leave the storehouse."

The two boys scrambled down the ladder and hid behind some bushes. They waited until their mother had left and then started to walk home.

"If our mother is a witch," Wild Boy said, "we should kill her. It won't do to have a witch living in our lodge."

"No, indeed," the other boy said.

The boys found heavy branches to use as clubs and went into the lodge, where Selu was waiting for them.

"I know what you are thinking," she said, "and I can't stop you from carrying out your plan. But if you are wise, you will follow my instructions. When you have killed me, go outside the lodge and clear a big, circular patch of ground. Drag my body around the circle seven times. Then drag my body seven times across the middle of the circle. Stay up all night to watch, and in the morning, there will be plenty of corn for you to eat."

The boys then killed their mother with their clubs and cut off her head with a sharp knife. They put her head on top of the lodge, facing west.

"Keep a lookout for your husband," the boys said to Selu's head.

Then, they cleared a space in front of the lodge, but instead of clearing it thoroughly, they only cleared seven small patches, and this is why corn grows only in some parts of the world and not in others. The boys took Selu's body and dragged it around the circle, and wherever drops of her blood landed, young corn plants sprouted up.

But the boys didn't follow their mother's instructions properly. Instead of dragging her seven times, they only dragged her twice, which is why a crop of corn must be worked twice, and not just once. When that work was done, the boys sat down to keep watch over the corn that had sprouted in the clearing.

While the two boys were watching the corn, Kanati came home.

"Where is your mother?" he asked the two boys.

"She was a witch, so we killed her," Wild Boy said.

"Yes. We put her head up on the top of the lodge," Wild Boy's brother said.

Kanati looked up at the top of the lodge, and there he saw the head of his dead wife.

He became very angry and said, "I cannot stay here with you. You don't know how to behave. I am going to the Wolf people now."

Kanati began to leave the clearing, but before he had gone very far, Wild Boy turned himself into a little tuft of down and settled on his father's shoulder.

Kanati never noticed the piece of down but kept walking on until he arrived where the Wolf people lived. When he arrived, he found the Wolf people were already gathered together to have a council.

The chief of the Wolf people saw Kanati arrive and said, "Welcome, stranger. Won't you tell us why you are here?"

"I am here because both of my sons are very bad people," Kanati said. "Something must be done about them. In seven days, please go to my lodge and play ball with those boys."

"We will go," the chief of the Wolf people said.

When Kanati heard the chief's promise, he left the place of the Wolf people. But he didn't go back home; instead, he kept walking on.

Now, when Kanati said "go play ball," what he really meant was "go and kill the boys," and the Wolf chief understood this. Wild Boy, who was still on his father's shoulder in the form of down, heard everything that had been said, and he understood what "go play ball" meant too.

Wild Boy allowed himself to float away from his father's shoulder and be carried away by the smoke from the council fire. Up, up, up, he floated, right through the smoke hole in the lodge. He floated over the roof of the lodge and then settled on the ground.

Wild Boy changed back into his human form and ran back home as fast as he could.

"We are in big trouble," Wild Boy said to his brother when he finally arrived home. "Father went to the Wolf people and asked them to come here and eat us. I know what we need to do to get ready. Come with me."

Wild Boy and his brother went outside the lodge, where they ran around it in a wide circle. They ran many times, to make a trail that stayed in the soft ground. They didn't close the circle, but rather, left one small piece open on the side that faced the direction the Wolf people would be coming from. Then the boys made themselves many arrows. They grouped them into four bunches and placed each bunch at intervals around the outside of the circle. Then they took their bows and hid behind some trees to wait for the Wolves to come.

A couple of days later, the Wolves arrived. They didn't see the trail the boys had made around the lodge, but they did go in through the opening, just as Wild Boy had said they would. As soon as the Wolves went through that gap, a great fence of briars and branches grew up along the trail that the boys had trampled into the ground. The boys then took their bows and used the arrows they had staged earlier to start killing the Wolves, who could not jump over the fence because it was too high. A few of the Wolves managed to escape through the opening and ran into the nearby swamp.

Wild Boy and his brother followed them, and when they reached the edge of the swamp, they both ran in circles around it. Wherever

Wild Boy and his brother ran, flames sprang up in their tracks. The fire burned its way into the swamp and killed all the Wolves except for two or three, who managed to escape. They became the ancestors of all the wolves that are in the world today.

The boys continued to live at their parents' lodge, harvesting the corn that grew up in the clearing and hunting for game in the forest. They sometimes made bread from the corn, and soon other people began to hear of the wonderful bread that these two boys made. One day, some strangers came to the lodge to speak to the boys.

"We have heard about your bread," the strangers said, "and we were hoping you would give us some."

"We'll do better than that," the boys said. "Here are seven grains of corn. Plant one every night on your way home, and watch over them all night. In the morning, you'll have plenty of corn that you can use to make bread for yourselves."

The strangers thanked the boys and returned home, a journey that took them seven days. At the end of the first day, they made camp and planted one of the seeds. They watched over the seed, and in the morning, seven tall stalks of corn were growing where the seed had been planted. They harvested the corn and went on their way. Each night when they made camp, they planted seeds of corn and watched over them, and each morning, even more corn was growing for them to harvest.

Now, the journey home was a long and weary one, and after five nights without sleep, the people were very tired. They planted the corn but were not able to keep their eyes open. They fell asleep, and in the morning, they found that no corn had grown at all. They brought home all the corn they had harvested and showed the people how to plant and harvest it, but because they had failed to watch over the seeds every night, it now takes many months for a crop to grow and ripen—where before it took only one night.

By the time the strangers came to visit the boys, Kanati had been gone for many months and had not returned.

"I think we should try to find Father," Wild Boy said.

"Yes," his brother said. "Let's try to find him."

Wild Boy took a wheel and rolled it to the west. Not long after, the wheel came back. Wild Boy took the wheel and rolled it to the north and south, and each time the wheel returned. Wild Boy then rolled the wheel to the east. The boys waited and waited, but the wheel did not come back.

"That is the direction we must look," Wild Boy said, so the brothers made ready and then set out eastward to find their father.

After many days of walking, the boys saw Kanati walking up ahead, with a small dog at his heels. The boys knew for certain that this was Kanati because the little dog was the wheel they had rolled. When it found Kanati, it turned itself into a dog and followed him everywhere.

The boys ran up to Kanati. Kanati stopped and looked at them.

Then, he said, "You are very bad boys. What are you doing here? Why are you following me?"

"We are men, and we go where we please," the boys replied.

"Do you intend to travel with me?"

"Yes."

"Very well. You may travel with me. But you have to go wherever I lead you."

The boys agreed, and so the three of them resumed their journey. After a time, they came to the edge of a swamp.

"Don't go in there," Kanati said. "There's something very dangerous that lives in that swamp."

Kanati resumed his journey, but the boys halted for a bit at the edge of the swamp.

"Let's go see what's in there," Wild Boy said. "I bet it's not half as bad as Father says it is."

The boys went into the swamp. They hadn't gone far when they found a giant panther, asleep. The boys took their bows and shot many arrows into the panther, but they could not kill it, and the panther paid them no attention. The boys gave up and left the swamp.

They caught up with Kanati, who said, "Well, did you find the dangerous thing?"

"We did. But it didn't hurt us at all, because we are men and we are not afraid."

Kanati was surprised by this news, but he didn't say anything. Instead, he resumed his journey, and the boys followed him.

After more walking, Kanati stopped and pointed. "See that place over there? That's a place where cannibals live. You want to stay away from there because if you go near, the cannibals will catch you and eat you."

Of course, no sooner had the words left Kanati's mouth than the boys wanted to go and see the cannibal village. They headed in the direction Kanati had indicated, and on the way, they came across a tree that had been struck by lightning.

"Take some of those burnt splinters," Wild Boy told his brother. "They'll come in useful later. I'll tell you what to do with them on our way to the cannibal village."

It didn't take long before the cannibals saw the two boys approaching. They ran up to the boys, captured them, and brought them back to their village.

"Everybody come and see what fine, fat boys we have caught!" the chief of the cannibals said. "Tonight, we eat well. Prepare for the feast!"

The cannibals made a great fire and put a big cauldron full of water over it. When the water was boiling, they grabbed Wild Boy and put him into the pot and put on the lid. But before Wild Boy went into the water, his brother knelt and put the splinters he had gathered from the tree into the fire. Then the cannibals put the other boy into the pot as well.

After some time, the chief of the cannibals said, "I think the meat should be ready now. Let's eat!"

All the cannibals gathered around, bowls at the ready to get their share. The chief took the lid off the pot, but instead of a nicely boiled dinner, a great ball of lightning was inside. The lightning exploded out of the pot, bolts flying everywhere. The lightning struck all of the cannibals, and soon they were all dead. Then the lightning gathered itself together and went up and out of the smoke hole. When the lightning disappeared, Wild Boy and his brother were standing there in the middle of the village as if nothing had happened.

The boys went looking for their father, and soon they caught up to him. Kanati was very surprised to see them.

"What, you're still alive?" he said.

"Of course we are," the boys said.

"Didn't you find the cannibal village?"

"Yes, we did, but we are men, and we are not afraid, so they did us no harm."

Kanati asked no more questions, but instead resumed his journey, and the boys followed him. This time, though, Kanati began walking very fast, and the boys couldn't keep up with him. They followed his trail, which ended at the place where the sun rises, at the very edge of the world. There the boys found Kanati and Selu.

"Come and join us," Selu said. "You can rest here a while, but you can't stay. This isn't a place for you. Your place is in the west, where the sun goes down. After you have rested, you need to go to the western edge of the world, which will be your new home."

The boys stayed with their parents for seven days, and then they set out for the edge of the world where the sun sets. They talked together as they walked along, and people far away heard their conversations, which sounded to them like the rumbling of thunder. The boys kept walking until they got to the edge of the world where the sun sets, and there they made their home.

Now, after the boys let all the animals and birds out of the hole in the mountain many years earlier, life became very hard for the people. There came a time when even the best hunters came home empty-handed, day after day.

"We will starve if this goes on much longer," the people said. "What can we do?"

One wise man said, "Send someone to the west to get the Thunder Boys. They'll be able to help us."

Messengers went to the Thunder Boys to ask for help. The boys readily agreed, and they journeyed to the place where the people lived.

When they got there, they said to the people, "We will call the deer for you. Have your bows ready."

Then the boys went into the townhouse, where the people had their feasts and their councils, and they began to sing. The boys sang their first song, and a sound like a roaring wind came from the northwest. The boys kept singing, and the noise got louder with each song. Just as the boys began their seventh song, a whole herd of deer came out of the forest. The people stood ready with their bows, as they had been told to do, and soon they had killed many deer, enough to feed the people for a long time.

The boys then said to the people, "We need to go back to our home. Once we get there, you will never see us again, but before we go, we will teach you our songs so that you can call the deer yourselves."

The boys taught the people all seven songs, but as the years passed, the songs became forgotten, all except for two, and these are the songs hunters still sing today when they want to catch deer.

The Tlanuwa and the Uktena

The Tlanuwa were great birds of prey that lived long, long ago. Their bodies were as long as a man is tall, and their wingspan was huge to match. They had sharp beaks and long talons, and they flew over the land every day looking for food for themselves and their young. The Tlanuwa were not particular about what they ate. Dogs would do just as well as deer, and if other animals weren't available, the Tlanuwa would swoop down and snatch up human children and bring them back to their nest to eat.

The Tlanuwa made their nest along the Little Tennessee River, on a high cliff where there was a cave. The cliff was sheer up to where the cave was, and the cave was protected from above by a rocky overhang that prevented anyone from climbing down to the nest. The people longed to rid themselves of these monstrous birds, but no matter how they tried, they were unable. Many brave men tried to climb up the cliff, but none could make it to the nest. Next, they tried waiting on the riverbank, bows at the ready. They shot arrows at the birds when they flew out to hunt, but it was no use: the arrows merely bounced off the birds' feathers.

Finally, the people went to the wisest medicine man they knew.

"Please help us," they said. "The Tlanuwa have taken so many of our children, and they're eating all the deer. Soon we will have neither children nor food, and we will die of starvation and sorrow."

"I know of the Tlanuwa," the medicine man said. "And I think I know how to deal with them, but I will need some of you to help me."

Several of the men readily agreed to help, and so the medicine man started the work he needed to do to prepare for his attack on the Tlanuwa's nest. First, the medicine man took strips of linn bark and made a long rope out of it. At the end of the rope, there were loops that he could put his feet into. Then he took a sturdy branch and carved it into a staff with a hook on one end. When the rope and staff were complete, the medicine man and his helpers climbed up to the top of the cliff, where they waited until the adult birds left to go hunting.

As soon as the adult birds left the cave, the medicine man told his helpers to hold the rope, and lower him down slowly, and then wait for him to tug on the rope to let them know he was ready to be pulled back up. The medicine man put his feet into the loops, and his helpers lowered him slowly and carefully over the edge of the overhang. Then the medicine man began to swing himself on the rope, back and forth, until he could hook his staff onto part of the wall of the cave where the nest was. Using the staff, he pulled himself onto the shelf and went over to the nest.

Inside the nest were four chicks. They had hatched only a few days ago, and so were still quite small, only about as big as a baby deer. The medicine man grabbed the nestlings one by one and threw them into the river below, where they were eaten by the Uktena, a great serpent who lived in the water. No sooner had the Uktena swallowed the nestlings than the medicine man saw the two parent birds flying back to the nest. He tugged on the rope, and his helpers pulled him back up just in time.

The Tlanuwa were very angry to find their nest empty. They flew out of the cave and circled in the air high above the river, screaming their rage into the sky. In the river below, the Uktena heard the noise the Tlanuwa were making, so he poked his head out of the water to see what was going on. The Tlanuwa saw the Uktena, and they immediately swooped down and snatched up the great snake in their talons. They ripped the Uktena to shreds in midair, and wherever a piece of the snake's body landed, it carved a hole in the rock. Those holes are still there today.

Two Tales of Snake Transformations

The Snake Boy

Once there was a boy who was the best in the village at hunting birds. Whenever he went out, he always came back with plenty of birds, which he would give to his grandmother. Everyone else in the village was jealous of the boy, both of his skill and of the fact that he would only share his catch with his grandmother. The villagers treated him so spitefully that he resolved to leave his village forever.

On the morning that the boy decided to start his journey, his grandmother prepared breakfast for him, but he would not eat.

"I can eat nothing today, Grandmother," he said, "because I am going on a great journey, and I need to fast so that I will be ready for whatever happens. But you must not grieve—I will be going somewhere safe, and I will be well. I love you always."

The boy then went out into the forest, where he spent the day.

In the evening, he returned with a pair of deer antlers he had found in the woods. Instead of going home, he went inside the winter house, where he found his grandmother waiting for him.

"Grandmother, I must sleep alone here tonight," the boy said.

The grandmother was sad, but she left the boy alone as he wished and went to sleep in another of her family's houses.

At daybreak, the grandmother rose and went to the winter house where her grandson had slept. She peeked through the door and what should she see but an enormous serpent, with horns on its head and two human legs!

"Grandmother, do not be afraid," the serpent said. "It is I, your grandson. I beg you to leave now. You have already seen too much."

The grandmother stepped away from the door but kept watch over the winter house. Many hours passed. When the sun was high in the sky, the door of the winter house opened, and a great uktena came slithering out. The uktena was so big that it took an hour for it to exit the house completely.

After the uktena left, it went through the village, hissing as it went. All the villagers were frightened and ran away, except for the grandmother, who knew who the uktena really was. The uktena slithered its way through the village and went down to the river, where it slid into the water and disappeared. The great serpent was so heavy that it left behind a deep channel in the ground along the path that it had taken.

The grandmother was heartbroken that her grandson had turned himself into an uktena and had gone to live in the river. She mourned for a very long time, and finally, the rest of the family became very impatient with her sadness.

"You saw where he went," they said. "If you miss him that much, why don't you throw yourself into the river and join him?"

"Very well," the grandmother said.

She left the village, following the track the serpent had made with its body. She arrived at the riverbank, but she never stopped walking. She walked into the water and kept walking until she disappeared into the deep running water.

Now, that was not the last time the people saw the grandmother. One day, a fisherman was casting his net on the riverbank, and he happened to look toward a large rock that rose out of the water a little way downstream. There he saw the grandmother, looking as she always did, sitting on the rock in the sun. As soon as the grandmother noticed the fisherman staring at her, she jumped in the water and was gone.

The Snake Man

Two hunters left their village early in the morning to see whether they might find some game to bring home. They followed many tracks and moved quietly, but no matter where they went, they found nothing but squirrels.

"I'm hungry," one hunter said, "and I swear those squirrels are taunting me. I'm going to catch some of them and have a fine feast tonight."

"Don't do it!" his companion said. "You know it's forbidden to eat squirrels. Something terrible will happen to you if you do."

"Nothing is going to happen. That's just a tale they made up to frighten children. I'm going to dress these squirrels and roast them, and then I'm going to eat them. There's plenty for both of us if you want to join me."

"No, thank you. Sometimes tales that are made up to frighten children actually mean what they say. I'd rather go hungry than find out what would happen if I ate squirrel."

The hunter laughed. "All right. Suit yourself."

The hunter proceeded to dress and cook the squirrels, which he ate hungrily. Meanwhile, his companion laid down and made ready for sleep. His back was turned to his friend so that he wouldn't be tempted to eat the squirrels too. It was hard to resist because the sizzling meat smelled so good, but the companion was steadfast, and eventually, he went to sleep—even though his stomach rumbled with hunger.

In the middle of the night, the companion was roused by the sound of agonized groaning. He opened his eyes and sat up, and on the other side of the fire, he saw his friend, writhing and moaning in agony. But that wasn't all: the hunter's legs had already stuck themselves together and were covered with shining green scales. He was turning into a giant serpent!

The companion watched in horror as his friend slowly turned into a giant serpent. There was nothing he could do to help, and soon the transformation was complete. In the place of the hunter, there was a great water snake. The snake looked once at the companion and then slithered off into the river. It was never seen again.

The Daughter of the Sun

As everyone knows, the Sun lives on the other side of the vault of the sky, but her daughter lives below it, right in the middle. Every day, the Sun climbs the great vault of the sky, starting in the east, and then she walks down the other side and goes to sleep in the west. When she gets to the middle of the sky, she likes to stop and visit with her daughter, and they share a meal.

Now, the Sun loved her daughter very much, but she wasn't as fond of the people who lived down on the earth.

One day, she couldn't bear it any longer, so she complained to the Moon, "Those people are just so ugly. Every time they look at me, they scrunch up their faces and squint. None of them will even bother to look at me properly. It's terribly ungrateful, considering all I do for them."

"I don't know what you're talking about," the Moon said. "Whenever they look at me, they smile. I find the people quite pleasant indeed."

Upon hearing that the Moon received such greetings from the people, Sun's jealously grew stronger. Finally, she decided that the best way to solve the problem would be to kill all the people. Every day, as she got close to her daughter's house, she sent down rays that carried a fever. Soon all the people were very sick, and many of them died. But still, the Sun did not stop; she wanted to keep sending the rays until every last person was dead.

The people were very worried.

"Everyone in our village has lost a loved one," they said, "and more people are getting sick by the day. If this keeps up, soon there will be no more people."

The people didn't know what to do. They had no power to stop the Sun. They held a council, and it was decided that they would go and ask the Little Men for help. The Little Men had magic powers, and they were on friendly terms with the people.

When the Little Men heard what the Sun was doing, they said, "Oh, dear. There's really only one way you can save yourselves. You'll have to kill the Sun."

"We don't know how to do that," the people said. "We don't even know how to get up to her house."

"Don't worry. We know what to do. Send us two of your bravest warriors tomorrow morning, and we'll get your problem solved."

In the morning, the two bravest warriors went to see the Little Men. The Little Men changed the men into snakes. One became a hognose snake, while the other was turned into a copperhead.

"Go to the house where the Sun's daughter lives," the Little Men said. "The Sun goes there for a meal every day at noon. If you wait next to the door, you can bite her when she arrives. Then she'll die, and you'll be free of the fever."

The two snakes slithered up into the sky and waited near the house of the Sun's daughter. At midday, the Sun arrived. The hognose snake was first to strike, but the Sun's light was so bright that he was blinded. All he could do was flop over on his back and spit out smelly slime.

The Sun saw the snake and smelled the slime.

"Oh, you disgusting thing," she said and nudged it away from the door with her toe.

The copperhead was so frightened by what had happened to the hognose snake that he slithered back home without even trying to bite. The hognose snake followed later—when he woke up from his fainting spell.

The two men went to visit the Little Men the next day. They explained what had happened.

"The Sun was too powerful," they said. "We couldn't even get close to her. Change us into some other kind of snake, one that can get close to the Sun."

This time, the Little Men changed one man into an uktena, and the other into a rattlesnake. The two snakes slithered back up to the house of the Sun's daughter and lay in wait for the Sun. As midday neared, the two snakes became very anxious. The rattlesnake coiled itself up in readiness to strike.

"I'm not going to miss this time," he said. "I'm so fast that the Sun won't even know what hit her."

Suddenly, the Sun's daughter opened the door of her house and stepped outside to see whether her mother was coming. The rattlesnake was so on edge that he didn't even think to make sure whom he was biting. He struck as fast as lightning, and after only a few minutes, the Sun's daughter was dead.

"Look what you did!" the uktena said. "We were supposed to kill the Sun, not this young woman. What are we going to do now?"

The rattlesnake was so ashamed of his mistake that he couldn't even reply. He slithered back home and asked the Little Men to change him back into a man. The uktena went home, too; he didn't want to be caught near the house when the Sun found out that her daughter had been killed by a snake bite.

The Sun finally arrived at her daughter's house. There on the threshold lay the body of the young woman. The Sun tried to revive her, but it was too late. Her daughter was dead. The Sun went into her daughter's house and shut the door. The world instantly became dark, and it stayed dark because the Sun would not come out. Instead, she stayed inside the house, grieving for her dead child.

Now the people had a different problem to solve. The fever had gone away, but if the world stayed dark, the plants and animals would begin to die. Soon there would be no food. So, the people went to the Little People and asked for help again.

"Since you're the ones who killed the Sun's daughter, you must be the ones to bring her back," the Little Men said. "You need to send seven men to the Ghost Country to find the Sun's daughter and bring her home to her mother."

The people chose seven brave men to go to the Ghost Country. The Little Men gave each man a rod made of sourwood. They also gave the seven men one large box.

"Here is what you must do," the Little Men said. "When you get to the Ghost Country, you will find that the ghosts are all having a dance. The Sun's daughter will be there, and she will be dancing too. As the dance circle comes around to where you are, you must strike the Sun's daughter with your sourwood rods until she falls down. Then you must pick her up and put her in the box. Close the lid tightly and then bring her back to her mother. But remember: you must not lift the lid until you get to the house where the Sun is, or the young woman will be lost forever."

The men promised to follow the instructions carefully and departed for the Ghost Country.

When they arrived, they found that the ghosts were all having a dance, just as the Little Men said they would. The men watched the dance for a while, and when they picked out the Sun's daughter from among the dancers, they got ready to strike her. Each time she went past one of the men, they hit her with their rods, and soon she fell to the ground. The men rushed over to her, picked her up, and put her in the box. The men picked up the box and started the long walk back to the Sun's daughter's house, where the Sun still sat grieving and refusing to shine.

As the men walked along carrying the box, the Sun's daughter awoke. After discovering that she had been imprisoned inside a box, she could not open the lid.

She banged on it with her fist and shouted, "Let me out! Please let me out!"

The men refused to listen and just kept walking.

For the rest of the journey, Sun's daughter begged the men to let her out.

"Please let me out! I can't breathe in here. Or if you won't let me out, at least open the lid a little way so that some fresh air can get in."

As the men were approaching the Sun's daughter's house, the pleas of the young woman became so piteous that they relented.

"Surely it won't hurt to open the box just a crack," they said. "We're so close to her house, and she's in such distress."

The men put the box down and lifted the lid just the tiniest crack. They heard a fluttering sound from inside the box. Something flew out of the box and into the bushes. The men couldn't see what it was, but they heard the sound of a redbird calling from the bushes.

The men picked the box up and continued their journey, but when they got to the house and opened the box, it was empty. The soul of the Sun's daughter had turned itself into a redbird and flown away when the men opened the box. This was a disaster not only for the Sun but also for all people because if the men had followed the instructions and kept the box shut, it would have been possible for us to visit the Ghost Country and bring our loved ones back to life. But because they opened the box too early, whenever someone dies, they are gone forever.

Now, the men had stopped by the Sun's daughter's house on the way to the Ghost Country, to let the Sun know that they were going to try to get her daughter back. The Sun had been very happy when she'd heard that news and had waited with great excitement at the prospect of getting to see her daughter again. But when the men opened the box and found it empty, the Sun began to wail and weep great tears. She wept so much that the earth became flooded, and the people began to drown.

So, the people decided to send their most beautiful young men and young women to sing and dance for the Sun, hoping that the music and dancing would cheer her up so that she would stop crying and shine again. The young people sang and danced in the best way they knew how, but nothing they did seemed to make any difference. Finally, the drummer started playing a different way, and the Sun stopped crying. She looked up at the dancers and listened to the song.

She watched the dance for a little while, and then she smiled, having forgotten her grief.

The Ball Game of the Birds and Animals

There came a time when the animals challenged the birds to a ball game.

"This will prove that we're better than the birds," the animals said. "There's no way such small creatures can stand against us. Anyway, they're practically half feathers and no muscle at all. Beating them will be easy."

The birds accepted the challenge, and a place and time for the ball game were decided between Bear, who was the captain of the animal team, and Eagle, who was the captain of the birds.

All the animals and birds were very excited about the game. Bear boasted of his great strength.

"See how I can heave these big logs around like they weigh nothing?" he said. "If I can do that, then any bird who tries to get in my way will be tossed aside the same way."

Turtle said, "I have a hard shell. Nobody is going to be able to stop me. Any blows they strike will just bounce right off, and won't hurt me at all."

"I'm faster than any other creature," Deer said. "Just give me the ball, and I'll run right to the birds' goal. Nobody will be able to catch me."

Two little mice heard about the game and wanted to play too. They went to visit Bear to see whether they could join his team.

When Bear saw the two tiny creatures, he roared with laughter. "You? Play the ball game with us? No, indeed. You'd just get trodden underfoot and be no use to us whatsoever. You just watch from the sidelines and see how real animals play ball."

Now, the animals didn't think much of the birds' team, but the birds did have Eagle on their side. They also had Hawk and the great Tlanuwa. These birds were very strong and could fly very high and fast. They had heard Bear and the other animals boasting, but they paid it no mind. The birds held their peace, thinking that deeds were better than words and that the animals would soon regret having been so boastful.

On the day of the game, the birds and animals all gathered at the field that had been chosen for the game. As Eagle was gathering his players to give them one last bit of encouragement before the game started, he suddenly heard a very small voice coming from the grass around his feet.

"Excuse me," the voice said. "We'd like to play ball too. Can we be on your team?"

Eagle looked down and saw two tiny mice. "Why don't you go and ask the animal captain? After all, you're both animals, and neither of you has wings to fly with."

"We did ask the animal captain," one of the mice said. "And he was very rude to us. He won't let us play."

"Oh, that's a shame. Let's see if we can find a way to get you some wings, and you can play for our side."

Eagle and his team went looking for things to use to make wings for the mice.

"Hey, look what I found!" Hawk said. "Here's the hide from the drum we used at the dance last night. We can make wings out of this."

Eagle and Hawk worked together to make wings out of the hide and some canes they found. They tied it onto the first mouse's little paws, which is how the first bat was made.

"Here, fly up and test your wings," Eagle said. "I'll throw you the ball, and we'll see how well you can play."

Bat (for this is what we must now call the first mouse) flew up into the air, and Eagle tossed him the ball. Bat caught it easily, and no matter how hard the other birds tried to get him to drop it, he held it fast.

Eagle was very impressed. "You're very good, even though this is the first time you've played as Bat. I think we'll be glad you're on our team."

"What are we going to do about the other mouse?" Hawk said. "There's not enough of the hide left to make him some wings."

"What if we just stretch him a bit?" Martin said. "We'll make him longer and stretch the skin between his paws. Then he'll have wings too."

The second mouse agreed, and so four large birds each took one of the mouse's paws in their beak and pulled and pulled until the second mouse was quite stretched out, and a good deal of soft, thin skin had been created on his sides. This is how the flying squirrel was made.

"How about you try your wings now?" Eagle said, and so Flying Squirrel (for this is what we must now call the second mouse) skittered up the trunk of a tree. Eagle threw the ball into the air. Flying Squirrel leaped off the branch and caught the ball in his mouth, but instead of gliding to the ground, he glided to a high branch in a neighboring tree.

"You're very good too," Eagle said. "I'm glad you asked to be on our team."

When both teams were ready to play, the signal was given, and the game began. The animals had the ball first, but they didn't keep it for long. Bear lumbered toward the tree where Flying Squirrel was waiting and tossed the ball to Deer. But Deer never caught it, because Flying Squirrel glided down and grabbed the ball with his little teeth. Then Flying Squirrel tossed the ball to Hawk, and so the birds tossed the ball back and forth among their players. This went on for some time until one of the birds dropped the ball.

"Aha!" Bear said. "Once we get that ball back, you'll never hold it again!"

But Bear never touched the ball, because Martin swooped in and caught it. Then Martin tossed the ball to Bat, who caught it and began to fly toward the goal. Even though Bat was flying close to the ground, none of the animals could touch him, because he dodged and flittered this way and that so quickly that even Deer couldn't catch him.

Finally, Bat came within range of the goal and tossed the ball in, winning the game for the birds.

Thus, Bear, Deer, and Turtle went home very humbled indeed because, for all their boasting, they hadn't even touched the ball for the whole game. The birds praised Martin for his speed and quick thinking and gave him a gourd that he could live in as a prize for saving the game for them. This is why martins live in little houses even today.

How Disease and Medicine Came to Be

Back when the world was new, and everything had only just been created, all of the plants, birds, and animals could talk, just like people, and the people lived peacefully alongside all the other creatures. But the people had many children, and soon there were so many people that it became difficult for them to find enough food. They looked around them and saw that many birds, animals, and fish looked like they might be good to eat. Plus, their fur, feathers, and skins would be useful for clothing, making drums, and other things. So, the people invented bows and arrows, knives and spears, nets and fish hooks. They went about hunting the birds and animals and fishing in the rivers and lakes. Soon, the people had plenty to eat, and ample furs, feathers, and skins. However, the birds, animals, and fish were very frightened and angry about being hunted and killed every day.

One day, the bears decided to have a council to decide what was to be done about the threat posed by the people. When the time came for the council, they all gathered in the townhouse at the foot of Kuwahi Mountain, the Mulberry Place. Old White Bear was the oldest and wisest of the animals, so he led the council. One bear suggested they make war on the people, to make them stop hunting.

All the other bears agreed that this was the best plan, so they began to discuss how to go about it.

One bear stood up and said, "The people have bows and arrows, and those work very well for killing us, so let's make bows and arrows of our own and use them for hunting people."

"All right," White Bear said. "We can try that. Make a bow and some arrows, and we'll use that."

One of the bears went into the forest and found a sapling for the bow. Another bear allowed himself to be killed so that his guts could be used to make the bowstring. The bear who had proposed the bow and arrows was first to try the weapon. The bear took the bow and nocked an arrow to the string. He pulled the string back and loosed the arrow, but his long claws got in the way, and the shot went nowhere near the target.

"You should trim your claws," the other bears said, so they helped the archer bear trim his claws, and then the bear tried another shot.

This time the arrow hit the center of the target.

"Oh, this is marvelous!" one bear said. "We can make many bows and arrows and go hunt the people. Then they'll leave us alone."

"Yes, they might leave us alone," White Bear said, "but what will we bears do for food? We need to climb trees to find good things to eat, and we can't go about killing half of our people to use their guts for bowstrings. Someone else will have to find a solution."

All the bears went home.

The deer came to the townhouse next for their council. Their chief was called Little Deer.

"What shall we do about the people who hunt us and use our flesh for food and our skins for clothing?" he asked.

"I have an idea," one of the deer said. "We should tell the people that their hunters have to ask our forgiveness every time they kill one of us. Otherwise, we will give them rheumatism."

Little Deer and the others agreed that this was a good solution, so they sent messengers to the settlements where the people lived.

The messengers told the people, "When you hunt us, the hunter must ask the animal he killed for forgiveness. Every time a deer is killed, our chief, Little Deer, will be there. Little Deer is swifter than the wind, and no arrow or spear can touch him. He will ask the slain deer whether the hunter asked for pardon. If the deer says 'Yes,' Little Deer will leave without doing anything. But if the deer says 'No,' Little Deer will follow the hunter home and give him rheumatism, and soon that hunter won't be able to walk anymore. He will be in pain all the time."

The next creatures to hold a council were the snakes and fish. They decided to send the people bad dreams about slimy things and rotting fish.

"That way, they will never want to eat us, because we'll make them so disgusted," the snakes and fish said. "And sometimes, the dreams will be so bad that the people will get sick and die."

When the snakes and fish were done with their council, the birds, insects, and other small animals held theirs. The frogs complained about the people calling them ugly and kicking them, which made their backs spotty. The birds complained about the people shooting them with arrows and then plucking out their feathers and roasting them over a fire.

Then, the chipmunk spoke. "I don't think the people are all that bad. At least they don't bother my people or me."

This made the other animals so angry that they slashed at the chipmunk with their claws, and this is why chipmunks have stripes on their backs.

By the time the council was ended, the birds, insects, and small animals had decided to create many different diseases and send them to the people to make them sick. Some of the diseases could kill.

Now, for all this time, the plants had been listening to the animals' councils in the townhouse.

"We can't let the people die. They are our friends," the plants said. "We will let the people take our leaves, bark, and flowers to use for medicine so that they don't die of these awful diseases."

Thus, disease and medicine came into the world.

Although the plants gladly offer themselves up as medicine, they can no longer speak, so we have to find out what purpose they have by ourselves. The healers of the tribe can find out these purposes because they know how to listen to the plants' spirits, which tell them what to use for medicine.

Here's another book by Matt Clayton
that you might like

Bibliography

Bastian, Dawn Elaine, and Judy K. Mitchell. *Handbook of Native American Mythology.* Santa Barbara: ABC-CLIO, 2004.

Berk, Ari, and Carolyn Dunn. *Coyote Speaks: Wonders of the Native American World.* New York: Harry N. Abrams, Inc., 2008.

Brown, Virginia Pounds, and Laurella Owens. *Southern Indian Myths and Legends.* Birmingham: Beechwood Books, 1985.

Cherokee Nation, "History." Accessed 21 September 2020. https://www.cherokee.org/about-the-nation/history/.

Dale, Edward Everett. *Tales of the Tepee.* Boston: D. C. Heath & Co., [1920].

Judson, Katharine B. *Native American Legends of the Great Lakes and Mississippi Valley.* Dekalb: Northern Illinois University Press, 2000.

Lankford, George, ed. *Native American Legends: Southeastern Legends: Tales from the Natchez, Caddo, Biloxi, Chickasaw, and Other Nations.* Little Rock: August House, 1987.

Mooney, James. *Myths of the Cherokee.* Washington, DC: Government Printing Office, 1902.

Morris, Cora. *Stories from Mythology: North American.* Boston: Marshall Jones Company, 1924.

Pijoan, Teresa. *White Wolf Woman: Native American Transformation Myths.* Little Rock: August House Publishers, Inc., 1992.

Taylor, Colin, ed. *Native American Myths and Legends.* London: Salamander Books, Ltd., 1994.

Young, Richard, and Judy Dockrey, eds. *Race with Buffalo and Other Native American Stories for Young Readers.* Little Rock: August House Publishers, Inc., 1994.

9 781953 934079